# The Enigma Of the Codex Gigas

## Unveiling the Devil's Bible

**CCM WATERSTON-HILLIER**

**Listed & Published on www.interestingbooks.store**

# Check out other exciting titles

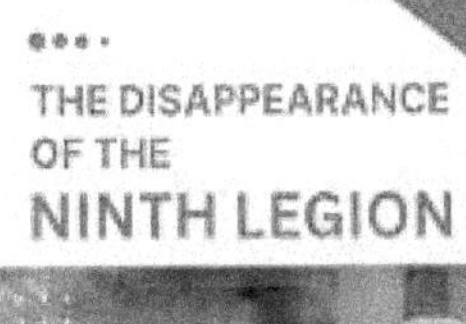


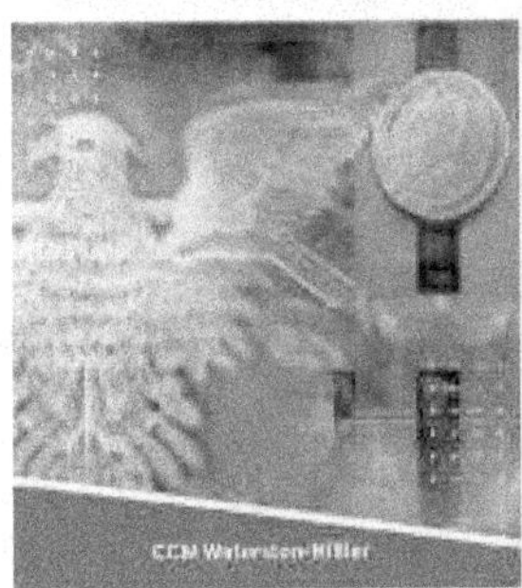

# Table of Contents

# FOREWORD

**Dear Reader,**

Welcome to *"The Enigma of the Codex Gigas: Unveiling the Devil's Bible."* This book is a journey through the history and mystery of one of the most fascinating relics of medieval times. The Codex Gigas, also known as the "Bible of the Devil," is an enormous manuscript that has captured the imagination of scholars and enthusiasts for centuries.

The Codex Gigas is a remarkable manuscript that has been the subject of much fascination and speculation over the years. It is a book shrouded in mystery, with a history as intriguing as the texts contained within its pages. The manuscript is believed to have been created in the early 13th century in a Benedictine monastery in Bohemia, now part of the Czech Republic.

It is a unique manuscript, not only because of its size but also because of the texts contained within its pages. The manuscript is over 3 feet tall and weighs over 165 pounds, making it one of the largest surviving medieval manuscripts in the world. It contains a variety of texts, including the Old and New Testaments, several other religious texts, medical treatises, and even a terrifying depiction of the devil himself.

The Codex Gigas is more than just a collection of texts. It symbolizes the ingenuity and creativity of medieval scribes, who painstakingly crafted this masterpiece over many years. The manuscript is believed to have been created by a single scribe who worked on it for over 20 years. The scribe is said to have been a monk sentenced to death for breaking his monastic vows. In a desperate bid to save himself, the monk offered to create a book that would contain all of human knowledge and be written in a single night. The monastery's abbot accepted the offer, and the monk began working. According to legend, the devil appeared to the monk and offered to help him complete the book in exchange for his soul. The monk agreed, and the devil helped him to finish the manuscript in a single night.

The Codex Gigas is a testament to the power of faith, the enduring human spirit, and a warning about the dangers of sin and temptation. The manuscript contains several religious texts, including the Old and New Testaments. These texts are a reminder of the importance of faith and religion's role in medieval society. The manuscript also contains several medical treatises, which are a testament to the ingenuity and knowledge of medieval physicians. These texts provide a glimpse into the medical practices of the time and the challenges physicians faced in treating various illnesses and injuries.

Perhaps the most intriguing text within the Codex Gigas is the depiction of the devil. This image is a striking and terrifying representation of the devil and is unlike any other depiction of the devil from the medieval period. The image is a reminder of the dangers of sin and temptation and the consequences that can result from giving in to these temptations.

In this book, we will explore the legend behind the Codex Gigas and delve into the pages of this remarkable manuscript. We will examine the texts within its pages, from ancient religious texts to medical treatises and even a terrifying depiction of the devil himself. We will also explore the history of the manuscript, from its creation in the early 13th century to its current location in contemporary libraries.

As you read this book, I hope you will be inspired by the story of the Codex Gigas and the people who created it. I hope you will gain a deeper appreciation for the rich history and culture of medieval Europe and the enduring legacy of this remarkable manuscript. The Codex Gigas is a testament to the enduring power of knowledge and the human spirit, and it is a reminder of the importance of preserving our cultural treasures for future generations.

Thank you for joining me on this journey of discovery.

**Sincerely,**

**CCM Waterston-Hillier**

# Chapter 1

# The Legend Begins

The legend of the mysterious manuscript unfolds. Rumors and whispers surround the Codex Gigas, also known as the Devil's Bible, capturing the imaginations of scholars, historians, and occult enthusiasts alike. Shrouded in secrecy, this ancient tome is said to possess supernatural powers and a dark history that has intrigued generations. As the legend begins, the reader is transported to a time long ago, when the Codex Gigas was first created and its enigmatic journey through the ages began. The tale weaves through medieval monasteries and hidden chambers, each custodian of the Devil's Bible adding a layer of mystique to its story. Some believe it was penned by a monk who made a pact with the devil, while others claim it was a desperate act of redemption. Regardless of its origins, one thing is sure: the Codex Gigas holds an extraordinary power within its pages that has fascinated and terrified those who dare to delve into its secrets.

# 1.1: Introduction to the Codex Gigas

It is 1295, and hidden behind the confines of a Benedictine monastery in Bohemia, an extraordinary book is being painstakingly written. A book of startling size is formed by its pages, composed of vellum and meticulously tied together. This is a page from the Codex Gigas, a document that would become famous in subsequent years as the "Bible of the Devil."

## The Enigmatic Manuscript

The Codex Gigas, often called the Devil's Bible, is an extraordinary relic of medieval history. It is not just a book; it is a legend, a mystery, and a symbol of both the sacred and the profane. This enormous handwritten document has dimensions of an astounding 36 inches in height, 20 inches in breadth, and more than 8 inches in thickness. Even today, this document's sheer size and weight make it an intimidating presence. Still, the physical characteristics of this book are not the only thing that has piqued the interest of researchers and fans alike.

The pages of the Codex Gigas have a wide variety of materials, including not only the Old and New Testaments of the Bible but also historical records, medicinal treatments, and even a terrifying depiction of the devil himself. These texts range from ancient to modern times and come from various cultures. The fascinating appellation given to the text is mainly because it contains both religious and secular information and the tales and stories surrounding its production.

## A Portal to the Past

The Codex Gigas is more than just a historical artifact; it is a gateway to the past that provides a peek into the thoughts of medieval scribes and the environment in which they lived. A narrative that spans millennia is told via the object's construction, contents, and the mysteries surrounding it. This story concerns commitment, artistry, and maybe even the devil's influence.

To get an understanding of the Codex Gigas, we need to go on a voyage through time, beginning in the Bohemian monastery of the Middle Ages, which is where it is said to have been made, and ending in the labs of the 21st century, where it has been the subject of scientific investigation. We will investigate the background of this mysterious manuscript, the legends and enigmas surrounding it, and the place this manuscript has in the realm of rare books and historical secrets.

As we embark on this journey of discovery, let us go back to the very beginning, to the point when the lore of the Devil's Bible was initially conceived inside the sanctified confines of a medieval convent.

# 1.2: The Early History of the Codex

## The Scribe's Herculean Task

The production of the Codex Gigas was not a routine endeavor by any means. It was a mammoth assignment that would have put even the most committed scribe to the test if they had attempted to complete it. A significant investment of time, effort, and perseverance was necessary to transcribe such a large amount of material. But who was the mastermind behind this colossal achievement, and what inspired them to take on such a challenging endeavor in the first place?

For a long time, academics have argued about the scribe responsible for the Codex Gigas. Some hypotheses imply that it was the work of a single person, while others see the potential of cooperation inside the monastery's scriptorium as a possible explanation. Regardless of the particulars, it is abundantly evident that the production of this document required a significant amount of toil and effort.

## Motivations Behind the Manuscript

Why exactly was the Codex Gigas compiled in the first place? This is one of the most critical issues about the Codex Gigas. What compelled the scribe (or scribes) to put in such a massive amount of work and effort to generate such a massive volume?

One notion that has gained much traction is that the writing was supposed to be some punishment. It is reported that a monk who resided at the Benedictine monastery in Bohemia was responsible for a severe crime that was so bad that it required extreme punishment, including being confined in a wall while still alive. As a last-ditch effort to avert this dreadful end, the monk proposed writing a book that would extol the virtues of the monastery and the holy precepts it upheld. This work would also serve as an act of remorse for the wrongs he had committed.

## Theological Significance

In addition to the performance of penance, the Codex Gigas is of paramount significance from a theological standpoint. It is a treasure trove of religious literature, one of which being the whole of the Latin Vulgate Bible, which was the translation of the Bible that the Catholic Church used throughout that period. Simply doing this task would have been a monumental feat for any writer.

However, adding the Bible is just the beginning of the project. Additionally, the manuscript includes a variety of religious literature, such as Josephus' "Antiquities of the Jews" and Isidore of Seville's "Etymologies." These writings are evidence of the scribe's (or scribes') aim to amass an exhaustive storehouse of information within a single book's confines, reflecting their wide-ranging interests.

As we delve further into the riddles of the Codex Gigas, we will investigate its background to find solutions to the problems that have perplexed academics and historians for generations. What inspired the production of this unique handwritten document, and what mysteries may be hidden inside its pages?

## 1.3: Myths and Mysteries

### A Pact with the Devil

Even though the physical characteristics of the Codex Gigas and its theological importance are both intriguing in their own right, the tales and stories that surround this document are the ones that have caught the imagination of the general public.

One of the most persistent and fantastic traditions connected with the Codex Gigas is the idea that it was constructed in a single night with the devil's help. This is considered one of this myth's most incredible aspects. According to the story, the monk who was responsible for transcribing the document quickly recognized that he would not be able to finish the arduous work within the time limit set. In desperation, he struck a deal with the devil to finish the manuscript in return for his soul. He would give up his life to finish the book in this deal.

According to the story, the devil accepted the bargain and finished the whole Codex Gigas in a single night in a breathtaking demonstration of lightning-fast intelligence and devilish skill. In return, an image of the devil was included in the document, permanently solidifying the wicked alliance.

## The Devil's Portrait

The representation of the devil that may be seen inside the Codex Gigas is startling and unsettling. It portrays a humanoid with horns and wings that has a threatening look on its face. The appearance of Satan in the devil is unlike any of the other images of Satan seen in religious art. This devil is represented with a pale complexion and a malicious, knowing smile rather than the conventional flaming red skin and pitchfork. Instead, he has a pitchfork in his hand.

The appearance of this image of the devil raises more problems than it answers. Using such a picture in a sacred text begs the question: Why? What exactly was the meaning behind it symbolically? Was it intended to demonstrate the urban legend that the devil was involved in producing the Codex Gigas, or did it serve another purpose entirely?

## The Power of Legends

The tale of the sinister beginnings of the Codex Gigas has been passed down from generation to generation, giving the document a sense of mystique and intrigue that has endured over the years. It has also aroused considerable debate regarding the nature of the contract between the monk and the devil and the repercussions of such a bargain.

The event above has inspired this conjecture.

Even if recent research has called into question whether or not this mythology is actual, the capacity of this story to catch people's imaginations ensures that it will continue to have power. It relates to our interest in the supernatural, namely our infatuation with the concept of striking bargains with evil powers to accomplish remarkable feats.

While we dive more into the secrets of the Codex Gigas, we will continue to investigate the myths and stories surrounding it. We aim to differentiate between fact and fiction as we search for the reality beneath this perplexing text.

In the first chapter, we lay the groundwork for our investigation of the Codex Gigas by providing an overview of its physical characteristics, the likely origins of the book, and the fascinating mythology surrounding it. We will explore more into the history of the book, its content, and the continuing riddles that make it one of the most interesting artifacts of the medieval world in the following chapters.

•◆◆◆◆◆◆◆◆•

# Chapter 2

# A Monumental Manuscript

Chapter 2 delves into the Codex Gigas as a monumental manuscript, examining its physical characteristics, historical context, and significance. This chapter explores the size and weight of the manuscript, its intricate illustrations and calligraphy, and the materials used in its creation. Additionally, it delves into the historical context in which the Codex was produced, shedding light on the cultural and intellectual environment that influenced its creation. Finally, this chapter discusses the manuscript's significance as a cultural artifact, considering its impact on history, theology, and art.

## 2.1: The Physical Characteristics

The Codex Gigas is a tribute to the artistry of a bygone period, and it may be found in the dimly lit hallways of libraries and museums worldwide. Because of its enormous size and weight, it projects an intimidating presence that commands respect and awe from all who encounter it.

Despite this, the Codex Gigas reveals much information about its creation, its authors, and the environment in which it was formed via its physical qualities and the information contained within its texts.

## The Size and Dimensions

When one first sees the Codex Gigas, they are immediately struck by its enormous size. It is one of the most significant medieval manuscripts preserved, with 36 inches in height (almost 3 feet), 20 inches in breadth, and a thickness of over 8 inches. The dimensions of the text are astounding. It is not only a question of curiosity about its proportions; they convey a tale about how practical and ambitious they are.

The Codex Gigas' length was not randomly selected while it was being created. Instead, it was a conscious choice by whomever or whoever created it to convey a specific message. In the days of the Middle Ages, when books were carefully created by hand, size was a symbol of importance. The more pages a book has, the more essential each chapter is. To put it another way, the Codex Gigas is a demonstration of the significance of itself.

## The Characteristics of Vellum

In addition to its enormity, another striking characteristic of the Codex Gigas' physicality is the superior quality of the vellum used to create it. Vellum, a writing medium created from animal skins, was highly regarded for its longevity and smooth surface, making it an excellent choice for the creation of manuscripts.

The vellum that was used in the creation of the Codex Gigas was of a highly superior grade. The meticulous care with which it was prepared is reflected in its pages' silky smoothness and excellent condition. No money was spared in producing this book because of the very high-quality vellum used. Additionally, it alludes to the renown and wealth of the monastery responsible for its production.

## The Intricate Binding

The physical qualities of the Codex Gigas extend to its binding, which is an independent work of art in its own right. The manuscript has a wooden cover wrapped in leather and secured shut with metal clasps. The cover itself is made of wood. The beautiful metalwork and detailed decorations on the cover reflect the artistry prevalent during that era.

Not only does the process of tying the Codex Gigas have a functional purpose, but it also serves a symbolic one. This aspect of the artifact reflects the reverence with which the text was treated. This was not a book to be read for pleasure; it was a holy relic, a priceless treasure that must be guarded and kept safe.

## Understanding That Can Be Felt

One has to connect with the Codex Gigas on a tactile level to have a genuine appreciation for it. One acquires a more excellent knowledge of the artistry and commitment that went into the production of the object by running their fingertips over the vellum pages, feeling the weight of the cover, and tracing the shapes of the metal clasps on the object with their fingers.

Rare manuscripts, such as the Codex Gigas, have several distinctive traits, one of which is a palpable link to the past. It allows us to bridge the gap between the medieval scribes who carefully copied its content and the current readers interested in deciphering its riddles.

# 2.2: Construction of the Tome

## The Challenges of Medieval Scribes

The production of the Codex Gigas was an enormous undertaking due to the volume of work involved and the complex technological obstacles it presented. The production of such a vast book presented the medieval scribes with numerous challenges, and their level of knowledge was tested at each stage of the process.

**Parchment Preparation:** In the beginning of making the Codex Gigas, one of the difficulties that had to be overcome was the preparation of the parchment. Animal skins, most often those of sheep, goats, or calves, are used to produce parchment. To make these skins into a writing surface that was fit for use, they needed to be scraped, treated, and meticulously cleaned.

The making of parchment needed a high level of expertise and prior knowledge. The skins needed to be pulled taut and then rubbed down to produce a smooth, even surface. Any faults or inconsistencies in the parchment might negatively impact the text's readability and ability to last over time.

**Mating of Ink:** Manufacturing ink was another essential component in creating manuscripts. The scribes created the ink used in the Middle Ages by combining several ingredients, including water, soot, and binding agents such as gum or egg white. A high level of accuracy and an understanding of the process of manufacturing ink were necessary to achieve the desired hue and consistency.

**Detailed Transcription:** The process of copying the text onto the vellum was both laborious and time-consuming. Quill pens, manufactured from bird feathers and dipped in ink, were used by scribes to write each letter and phrase painstakingly. The accuracy required for this job was very high, and the possibility of making mistakes was always there.

## Craftsmanship Exposed as It Is

The difficulties that the medieval scribes encountered in constructing the Codex Gigas shed light on the high degree of artistry and commitment necessary for an endeavor of this magnitude. Each page of the book shows the scribe's prowess and meticulous attention to detail.

The fact that the Codex Gigas was printed by hand rather than using any of the sophisticated printing methods available today .adds to the importance of its historical status. It is a physical connection to a period when books were uncommon and valuable commodities manufactured via a rigorous and careful process. In that era, creating a book required much time and effort.

As we delve further into the making of the Codex Gigas, we develop a tremendous respect for the skilled artistry of the medieval scribes responsible for bringing it to life. The tale of how this unique text came to be includes the scribes' devotion to the preservation of information, their mastery of the materials they worked with, and dedication to their trade.

In Chapter 2, we dig into the many physical aspects of the Codex Gigas, such as its dimensions, the caliber of the vellum it was written on, and the complexities of its binding. In addition, it examines the difficulties that medieval scribes had while making such a large and complex book, demonstrating the level of artistry and commitment necessary for such a gigantic endeavor. In the following chapters, we shall continue with our investigation into the riddles as well as the history of the Codex Gigas.

# Chapter 3

# The Art of the Devil

This chapter focuses on the art and symbolism associated with the devil. It examines the intricate illustrations and illuminations throughout the manuscript that depict various representations of the devil and his domain. Readers are taken on a visual journey through the dark and captivating world of demonic imagery, showcasing the mastery and creativity of the manuscript's creators.

## 3.1: The Devil's Portrait

Within the pages of the Codex Gigas, between the religious scriptures and historical records, a remarkable picture has grabbed the imagination of centuries of people: the notorious depiction of the devil. This unnerving representation stands in sharp contrast to the religious and intellectual information that surrounds it, which raises the issue of why such a menacing figure would find a home in a sacred document in the first place.

19

## A Startling Image

The image of Satan that may be seen in the Codex Gigas is quite terrifying. This horned and winged creature with burning eyes and a frightening smile is unlike any standard portrayal of Satan seen in works of religious art. The depiction of the devil in the book is ghostly white, and its features are angular and pointed, giving off an impression of hostility.

Within the Codex Gigas is a painting of the devil that takes up a whole page and is accompanied by a cryptic, condensed passage of writing. The prominence of the picture in the overall composition of the book is highlighted by the ornate borders and patterns surrounding it. We must investigate the symbolism and iconography connected with the devil in medieval art to have any hope of comprehending the existence of this satanic picture.

## The Use of Iconography and Symbolism

In both the religious and secular cultures of the Middle Ages, depictions of the devil were commonplace and inspired a healthy amount of terror. His part had several facets and touched on various topics, including temptation, sin, and damnation. Scribes and artists often communicated these ideas via symbolic imagery, and the depiction of the devil was widespread in medieval art.

The depiction of the devil in the Codex Gigas may be

comprehended when placed within the framework of demon imagery from the Middle Ages. Typical attributes associated with Satan include horns, wings, and a devilish look. Incorporating these characteristics into the Codex Gigas is consistent with the more general artistic traditions that prevailed during this era.

**A Warning and Reminder:** One potential meaning of depicting the devil in the Codex Gigas is that it acts as a word of caution to the person reading it. From a theological perspective, the devil is seen as the greatest tempter, who draws people away from the road leading to righteousness. Including a picture of the devil in the book may have been done to warn the reader about the ever-present threat posed by sin and temptation.

The unpleasant appearance of the devil would have brought attention to the terrible character of the temptations being offered. The fact that it is found inside the pages of a sacred document may serve as a sharp warning of the repercussions of deviating from the road that leads to righteousness.

## Questions of Motivation

The fact that the Codex Gigas contains a depiction of the devil raises issues about the intentions of whomever or whatever created it in the first place. Why would a picture that is both provocative and uncomfortable be included in a religious manuscript that is allegedly meant for spiritual purposes? According to a few schools of thought, this may have been done intentionally to highlight the stark difference between good and evil and righteousness and sin.

**A Cautionary Tale:** The Devil's image, according to one interpretation, is that the devil's portrait serves as a cautionary tale. It's possible that they wanted to show the repercussions of giving in to temptation and deviating from the road of faith through this illustration. When seen in this light, the picture of the devil may serve as a stern warning to the reader about the dangers of sinning and the significance of maintaining one's faith despite the challenges it may provide.

**A Display of Power:** Another hypothesis proposes that including the image of the devil was done as a display of the creator's strength, and this was the motivation for including the portrait. In the world of the Middle Ages, a scribe's creative skill would have been put to the test if they were capable of depicting the devil in a way that was both vivid and terrifying. It's possible that they did it to demonstrate how skilled they were in the trade.

## The Devil's Role in Medieval Theology

The devil's function in medieval theology and folklore must also be considered if we are to completely comprehend the devil's appearance in the Codex Gigas.

When people thought about things from a religious perspective during the time, the devil was seen as a genuine and dangerous entity. It was claimed that he continuously plotted against humanity and tempted people to win them over to his way of thinking.

**A Theological Adversary:** According to Christian theology, the enemy of God and humanity is represented by the devil. He was the personification of evil, the fallen angel who rebelled against God and endeavored to taint the universe that God had made. This theological viewpoint may have been meant to be reinforced by the picture of the devil seen in the Codex Gigas since the figure serves as a visual symbol of evil and seduction.

**Folkloric Fears:** The Devil was a significant character in medieval religion and medieval folklore. In the oral traditions that were prevalent during that time, accounts of meetings with the devil, pacts with demons, and supernatural occurrences were widespread. The picture of the devil included in the manuscript may have resounded with the fears and stories associated with folklore, which would have given the text a sense of both interest and caution.

## 3.2: Devil in the Middle Ages

To get a complete understanding of the Devil's function in the Codex Gigas, we need to investigate the broader cultural and historical backdrop of the Devil throughout the Middle Ages. During this period, the opponent of religion, the devil, was also a ubiquitous and multidimensional character in society. This was in addition to his role as a theological antagonist.

## The Medieval Perception

During the Middle Ages, the clergy and the public saw the devil as a pivotal character in their understanding of the universe. It was widely believed that he existed perpetually and continuously incited people to disobey God and indulge in sinful behavior. This all-pervasive sense of the devil's presence was bolstered via various mediums, including sermons, religious texts, and artistic creations.

**Fear and Dread:** The depiction of the devil in medieval art and literature often inspired the audience's feelings of horror and dread. His evil influence manifested itself in the form of natural calamities, sicknesses, and moral degeneration. It was widely believed that the devil was not only an abstract notion but an actual, material power active in the broader world.

**The Devil in Art:** The depiction of the devil throughout the Middle Ages often took on several guises. The devil was often depicted in religious writings and artworks as a hideous, horned creature with sinister facial characteristics. These images emphasized the devil's evil character and the significance of avoiding succumbing to his temptations.

## The Devil's Role in Medieval Theology

In medieval Christian theology, the devil was given tremendous attention. He was believed to be the most potent enemy God and humanity could ever face. He was also considered the personification of sin and evil. The study of the devil and his strategies received significant focus from the religious community.

**Temptation and Sin**: According to Christian theology, the fundamental function of the devil is that of the tempter. It was thought that he would tempt people to engage in sinful behavior, diverting them from the road leading to virtue. This theological stance emphasized how important it is to avoid giving in to temptation and to keep one's faith unwavering at all times.

**Hell and Damnation:** The dread of damnation and everlasting punishment in hell was a potent motivation in medieval Christianity. This fear was especially prevalent in the Middle Ages. As an additional means of driving home the point that sin had severe repercussions, the devil was often portrayed as a torturer of souls in hell. It's possible that seeing a picture of the devil in the Codex Gigas acted as a sharp reminder of these important religious concepts.

## Folklore and Legends

In addition to the religious beliefs of the time, the devil was also a significant figure in the folklore and stories of the Middle Ages. The public imagination was filled with tales of people having run-ins with Satan, agreeing with evil spirits, and experiencing otherworldly occurrences.

**Faustian Bargains:** One of the most enduring legends of the Middle Ages was the Faustian bargain, in which individuals made deals with the devil in exchange for worldly power or knowledge. The Faustian bargain is considered to be one of the most lasting legends. These stories were often told to act as cautionary tales, to educate listeners about the perils of greed and ambition.

**Encounters with the Supernatural:** There are a lot of tales in medieval mythology about people having supernatural encounters with the devil. In several of these stories, the devil is shown as using a variety of guises to lure people astray and trick them. The devil's cunning and power to sway human impulses were recurring motifs throughout these tales.

## The Devil's Place in the Codex Gigas

Including a picture of the devil in the Codex Gigas takes on a more significant meaning when seen in the larger context of the beliefs and culture prevalent throughout the medieval period. It depicts the ubiquitous and diverse role that the devil played in medieval culture, from theological perspectives down to folkloric beliefs. Sin, temptation, and the never-ending battle between good and evil are all significant theological and cultural concepts, and the devil's figure serves as a visual depiction of these ideas.

As we continue our investigation of the Codex Gigas, we will dig even deeper into the mysteries surrounding this incredible document. The depiction of the devil is only one layer of the many mysteries in the Devil's Bible. As we go further into its pages and history, we will find many more layers to unravel.

The appearance of a picture of the devil inside the Codex Gigas is investigated in Chapter 3. This chapter also delves into the symbolism and iconography of the devil in medieval art and religion. In addition to this, it sheds light on the broader cultural backdrop of the devil throughout the Middle Ages, highlighting this figure's diverse role in society, religion, and folklore. This chapter lays the groundwork for additional investigation into the mysterious contents of the manuscript as well as the book's ongoing mysteries.

# Chapter 4

# Echoes from the Monastery

This chapter explores the influence of medieval monasticism on the depiction of the devil in art and manuscripts. It delves into the specific practices and beliefs of monastic communities and how these influenced the portrayal of the devil as a tempter and adversary. Additionally, this chapter examines illuminated manuscripts' role in transmitting religious teachings and perpetuating medieval beliefs about the devil. Readers understand how monastic scribes and artists used visual representations to convey theological concepts and moral messages by analyzing specific illuminated manuscripts.

The intricate and detailed illustrations in these manuscripts often depicted the devil as grotesque and menacing, with horns, claws, and a sinister smile. These visual representations aimed to evoke fear and warn viewers of the dangers of succumbing to temptation. By studying these manuscripts, historians can trace the evolution of the devil's portrayal and understand the impact of religious teachings on medieval society's perception of evil. Ultimately, the illuminated manuscripts serve as a testament to the power of visual storytelling in shaping religious beliefs and moral values during the Middle Ages.

# 4.1: Monastery of Podlažice

To decipher the enigmas contained inside the Codex Gigas, we will need to go on an adventure through time to the Monastery of Podlaice, which is said to be the location where the mysterious text was first discovered. This monastery, which may be found tucked away in the medieval countryside of Bohemia, was an essential component in the production and maintenance of the Devil's Bible.

**Historical Background**

The Benedictine Monastery of Podlaice, commonly referred to as the Podlaice Abbey, was situated in the region now known as the Czech Republic. It was close to Podlaice, surrounded by undulating hills and thick woods. The isolated location of the monastery made for an excellent backdrop for leading a contemplative lifestyle and engaging in intellectual pursuits.

The establishment of the monastery may be traced back to the early part of the 13th century, which places it in the same time frame as the era in which the Codex Gigas is said to have been written. The pious monks who established the monastery were committed to pursuing religious truth via prayer and studying the canonical scriptures.

## The Role of the Monastery

In medieval Europe, monasteries played essential roles as centers of study, spirituality, and preserving cultural traditions. The Podlaice Monastery was not an exception to this rule. The monks who lived inside its sacred walls devoted their lives to studying knowledge, prayer, and copying and transmitting holy writings.

**Scriptorium and Transcription:** Transcribing manuscripts was an essential part of the monastic community's work. Thus, the monastery had a particular room dedicated to the task. Because no printing presses were available, book production had to be done by hand, and the centers of this labor-intensive activity were located in monastic scriptoria. Skilled monks would copy holy scriptures meticulously, generating new volumes or replicating existing ones.

It is thought that the Codex Gigas was written at the scriptorium of the Podlaice Monastery in Bohemia, which was also the location of the monastery. The herculean endeavor to transcribe such a vast document would have been carried out at this location. The devotion and knowledge of the monks who worked in the scriptorium were essential in producing the Devil's Bible.

**Spiritual Life and Devotion:** Monastic life was defined by a disciplined regimen that included prayer, reflection, and physical work. Devotion and spiritual life were closely intertwined. The monks of Podlaice Abbey were devout Christians who adhered to the Rule of Saint Benedict. This was a code of conduct that placed a strong emphasis on submission to authority, modesty, and prayer.

The production of sacred manuscripts was intricately entwined with the monastic community's devotional activity at the monastery. A devout deed as well as a method of disseminating God's word, the act of transcribing holy scriptures was considered to be of paramount importance. The considerable religious material in the Codex Gigas showed this dedication to maintaining spiritual traditions.

## The Alleged Connection

The Monastery of Podlaice is said to play an essential role within the lore surrounding the Codex Gigas. The legend has it that the Codex Gigas was written by a single monk inside these monastery walls as an act of penance; this monk took on the colossal job of writing the book to atone for his sins.

**The Monk's Grave Offense:** The story of the monk who committed the serious crime that led to the construction of the Codex Gigas is told in the tradition surrounding the production of the Codex Gigas. According to the narrative, the monk was excommunicated from the Monastery of Podlaice. According to the legend, the monk's misdeeds were so horrible that the abbot of the monastery found them to be so heinous that he condemned the monk to the destiny of being walled up alive behind the walls of the monastery, a fate that assured a protracted and excruciating death.

**The Desperate Bargain:** Confronted with such a dreadful end, the doomed monk attempted to strike a hopeless deal. He volunteered to write a book in a single night that would praise the monastery, include all of human knowledge, and serve as an act of penance for his transgressions. This book would be written in a single night. The monk offered to save himself from being executed in return for fulfilling this impossible mission.

The abbot, who was cautious about the monk's offer but fascinated by it, accepted the proposition. The monk was shut up in his cell with the required items for the transcription, and work then got on.

**The Supernatural Assistance:** According to the tradition, the monk toiled all through the night, trying to transcribe as much as possible. The passage of time made it abundantly evident that he could not do the work given to him. In despair, he sought aid from a sinister force—the devil himself—to solve the problem.

It is reported that the devil granted the monk's request

and finished the book's remaining pages in a single night. The diabolical agreement was continually solidified in the form of the enormous text known as the Codex Gigas, which included a terrifying depiction of the devil on one of its pages.

## Separating Fact from Legend

It is vital to approach the narrative of the creation of the Codex Gigas with a critical eye, even though the legend itself is intriguing. To a large extent, what we know about the creation of the text is dependent on subsequent narratives and traditions since historical documents from the period when the manuscript was made are very limited.

For a very long time, historians and other researchers have argued about whether or not the monk's narrative is true and whether or not supernatural powers were involved. Others contend that the mythology is the result of elaboration based on folklore. In contrast, others theorize that the story could conceal certain aspects of reality.

The Monastery of Podlaice is still a site of historical importance and mystery to this very day; it is also a location that will be inextricably tied to the myth of the Codex Gigas for all time to come. Whether the tale is merely a gripping story or contains the key to uncovering the secrets of the text, it continues to provide an aura of mystery to this astonishing relic from the world of the Middle Ages.

## 4.2: Monastic Life

We need to dive into the day-to-day activities of the monks who lived at the Monastery of Podlaice so that we may better understand the atmosphere that is said to have been there during the writing of the Codex Gigas. During the Middle Ages, monastic life was defined by prayer, labor, and devotion routines, all of which played an essential part in developing religious manuscripts. These routines also played a role in the preservation of religious texts.

**The Benedictine Rule:** The monks of the Monastery of Podlaice and many others in medieval Europe adhered to the Benedictine Rule. This collection of norms, which was developed by Saint Benedict of Nursia in the 6th century, detailed the fundamentals of monastic life and the associated behaviors.

**Obedience and Humility**: The values of obedience and humility were at the core of the Benedictine Rule. The monks were obligated to humble themselves before their abbot and subject themselves to his power over the monastery. The Rule placed a strong emphasis on maintaining a state of stillness, engaging in contemplation, and seeking out opportunities for spiritual advancement.

**The Daily Office:** The Divine Office or Liturgy of the Hours was an essential component of monastic life and is sometimes referred to by its other name, the Daily Office.

The monks' day was interrupted by a cycle of daily prayers, psalms, and readings, which shaped their daily activities around the rhythms of worship.

## Daily Routines

The routine activities of a Benedictine monk's day were highly disciplined and centered on striking a healthy balance between prayer, labor, and repose. These rituals served as a foundation for the monks' personal growth on a spiritual level as well as their contributions to the monastic community as a whole.

**Divine Office:** The first prayers of the Divine Office were traditionally said before dawn as the day would traditionally begin. These early morning prayers, referred to as Vigils or Matins, signaled the beginning of the liturgical calendar for the day.

**Manual Labor:** Following the morning prayers, the monks would begin their day with work by hand. This job was often connected to the upkeep of the monastery and included activities like farming, gardening, brewing, and transcribing manuscripts. The act of working was seen as a type of spiritual discipline and a chance for reflection at the same time.

**The Hours:** The monks convene at different times throughout the day to participate in the Hours of the Divine Office. These included Lauds, which is the prayer spoken in the morning; Prime, Terce, Sext, and None, which are prayers said at the third, sixth, and ninth hours of the day, respectively; Vespers, which is the prayer said in the evening, and Compline, which is the prayer said in the night.

**Silence and Contemplation:** The monastic life was characterized by a strict observance of silence, considered an essential component. Monks were required to follow a vow of silence whenever they were not participating in communal prayer or doing business. This exercise made it possible to engage in introspection and reflection, which helped to cultivate a profound feeling of spirituality.

## Religious Copying and Transcription

Copying and transcribing holy writings was an essential part of the monastic community's daily life and was one of the primary tasks inside the monastery. In the medieval period, monasteries were often used as stores of knowledge, and the monks who lived there played an essential part in preserving and disseminating written works.

**The Scriptorium:** Monastic scriptoria were specialized spaces inside monasteries dedicated to copying and illuminating manuscripts. Skilled monks, sometimes known as scribes, were responsible for the detailed hand transcription of holy scriptures—the procedure called for high accuracy, perseverance, and a profound dedication to the safekeeping of information.

**Illumination and Decoration:** In addition to their work as scribes, monks were also responsible for illuminating and ornamentating the manuscripts they worked on. They transformed the pages into art pieces by meticulously adding detailed patterns, pictures, and decorations.

## The Monastery as a Center of Learning

Not only were monasteries like Podlaice Abbey considered sites of religious devotion, but they were also considered centers of study and research. Theologians, philosophers, and scholars of ancient literature were among the subjects that monks studied. They accumulated information in the form of manuscript collections and stored it away in libraries that they had established.

The Monastery of Podlaice's dedication to learning and religious practice offers illuminating background information that helps comprehend how the Codex Gigas came into being. The book was said to be written in an atmosphere characterized by prayer, hard work, and a commitment to acquiring information; this was the setting.

In Chapter 4, we investigate the historical importance of the Monastery of Podlaice, which is said to be the spot where the Codex Gigas was first created. We dive into the routines of prayer and labor that the monks who inhabited the monastery followed, as well as their part in the transcription and preservation of sacred documents, as part of our exploration of their everyday lives. This newfound knowledge about the monastic way of life paves the way for deeper investigation into the text's origins and the mysteries surrounding it.

# Chapter 5

# Beyond the Bible

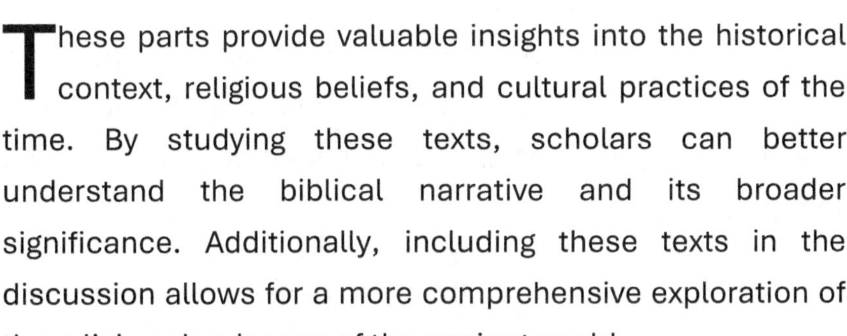

These parts provide valuable insights into the historical context, religious beliefs, and cultural practices of the time. By studying these texts, scholars can better understand the biblical narrative and its broader significance. Additionally, including these texts in the discussion allows for a more comprehensive exploration of the religious landscape of the ancient world.

## 5.1: Contents of the Codex

As we continue to explore further into the pages of the Codex Gigas, we come across a rich tapestry of passages that go much beyond the typical material of the biblical canon. This chapter delves into the many contents of the book, illuminating its religious, historical, and medicinal writings in the process. Each part provides a taste of this unique work's vast body of information.

## The Holy Bible: At the Center of It All

The Bible is at the center of the Codex Gigas. The Bible is a collection of religious literature that has influenced the beliefs and behaviors of innumerable people throughout human history. The Bible is placed in the text since it makes up many of the pages that make up the document.

**Old and New Testaments:** Both the Old Testament and the New Testament are included in the Codex Gigas, which makes it a complete collection of biblical writings because it includes both the Old Testament and the New Testament. The reader will encounter well-known tales, lessons, and passages that Christians have treasured for many decades.

**The Vulgate Translation:** The Bible version contained in the Codex Gigas is the Latin Vulgate translation of the Bible, which is credited to Saint Jerome. This version of the Bible was thought to be the definitive Latin text of the Bible during the Middle Ages because of its widespread usage and acceptance in medieval Europe.

## Pastoral and Liturgical Texts

In addition to the Bible, the Codex Gigas contains various writings used in pastoral and liturgical contexts. These works were necessary for the monastic community's religious life and would have been included in the monks' regular rites and practices as part of their everyday lives.

**Liturgical Calendar:** Calendar of the Liturgical Year The text includes a liturgical calendar, which served as a guide for the observance of various religious holidays and seasons throughout the year. This calendar offered the monks a framework for their religious exercises that were both ordered and organized.

**Psalms and Hymns:** Psalms and hymns occupied a pivotal role in the worship in monasteries. The Divine Office and other liturgical services would have included reciting or singing a collection of psalms and hymns in the Codex Gigas. These psalms and hymns may be found in the Codex Gigas.

## Historical Chronicles

In addition to its religious material, the Codex Gigas also contains historical chronicles that provide a look into the world of the Middle Ages. These books provide illuminating information on the period's historical figures, political systems, and cultural practices.

**Chronicle of Bohemia:** The Codex Gigas contains several critical historical manuscripts, including one called the Chronicle of Bohemia. This chronicle details the history of the Bohemian territories, providing an account of the kings and rulers that ruled the area, as well as the battles and other notable events that took place there.

**Other Historical Records**: The manuscript includes several other historical records and annals besides the

Chronicle of Bohemia. The period in which the Codex Gigas was compiled may be better understood with the help of the historical background provided by these works.

**Texts on Medicine and Traditional Treatments**

Unexpectedly, the Codex Gigas has a section about medical literature and treatments. This inclusion demonstrates the variety of information in the book and provides insights into the medical procedures prevalent throughout the medieval period.

**Treatises on Medical Issues**: The medical area of the library contains treatises on a variety of medical issues, including the treatment of ailments, the creation of medicines, and the qualities of herbs and medicinal plants. These works reflect the medical knowledge prevalent during that period, as well as the attempts made to reduce suffering and improve health.

**Herbal and Medical Illustrations**: Accompanying the various medical books are detailed pictures of plants and herbs. These drawings offer a visual layer to comprehend the many therapeutic characteristics. These pictures provide an exciting look into the botanical knowledge throughout the Middle Ages.

## 5.2: The Unusual Texts

As we go further into the Codex Gigas, we come across

documents that resist straightforward classification within the conventional framework of historical or religious manuscripts. These texts have not been preserved in any other form. These peculiar writings contribute to the mystique surrounding the book and raise fascinating concerns about the relevance and function of the texts themselves.

## The book is attributed to Josephus

The fact that the writings of Flavius Josephus, a Jewish historian who lived in the first century, are included in the Codex Gigas is one of the most notable aspects of this ancient book. The manuscript's religious and historical passages are displayed alongside Josephus's works, which record Jewish history and the Jewish-Roman War.

**A Unique Inclusion:** Josephus's writings are unusually absent from Christian religious documents from the period covered by the Codex Gigas, making their inclusion in this ancient book somewhat of a rarity. Scholars are baffled by its inclusion, which raises issues about the document's target audience and the reasons for its production.

## The Art of Exorcism

The Codex Gigas has a section specifically devoted to the art of exorcism, which is not often seen in the context of religious manuscripts. This assemblage of writings includes instructions and prayers for driving away demons and other evil entities.

**A Focus on Exorcism:** The Codex Gigas dives into a domain of spiritual activity that was sometimes considered beyond the mainstream of medieval Christianity. Yet, it gives the practice of exorcism a prominent place in the text. This is a rare occurrence. The presence of these works gives the impression that there was an interest in facing and overcoming supernatural powers.

## The Heptameron of Peter of Abano

The Heptameron of Peter of Abano is a grimoire, sometimes known as a book of magic spells and rituals, and it is one of the less traditional works included in the Codex Gigas. This work, said to have been written by the Italian philosopher and magician Peter of Abano in the 13th century, discusses calling forth angels and devils.

**A Mystical and Occult Dimension:** The inclusion of the Heptameron lends the work a mystical and occult dimension. It calls into doubt the philosophical and theological convictions of the scribe or scribes responsible for the Codex Gigas, and their interest in esoteric knowledge.

## The Significance of Diverse Content

The fact that the Codex Gigas contains such a broad collection of writings draws attention to the diverse character of the document as well as the varied interests of the people who created it. The document covers various topics, including spiritual devotion, historical knowledge, medical expertise, and even occultism in certain places. This variety reflects the intricate tapestry that was the intellectual and spiritual life of the Middle Ages.

As we continue our investigation of the Codex Gigas, we will dive further into these writings to decipher their meanings and understand the relevance of what they imply about the book. The Devil's Bible is a book that has always been shrouded in mystery, and each chapter provides a fresh perspective on the thinking and ideas that prevailed throughout its era.

This chapter dives into the many contents of the Codex Gigas, highlighting its religious, historical, medicinal, and even occult passages in the process. Incorporating these many elements gives the document a greater depth and complexity, which raises issues about the purpose for which it was created and the motives of those who created it. This chapter lays the groundwork for future investigation into the peculiar and mysterious elements of the Devil's Bible.

••••••••••

# Chapter 6

# Scribal Endeavors

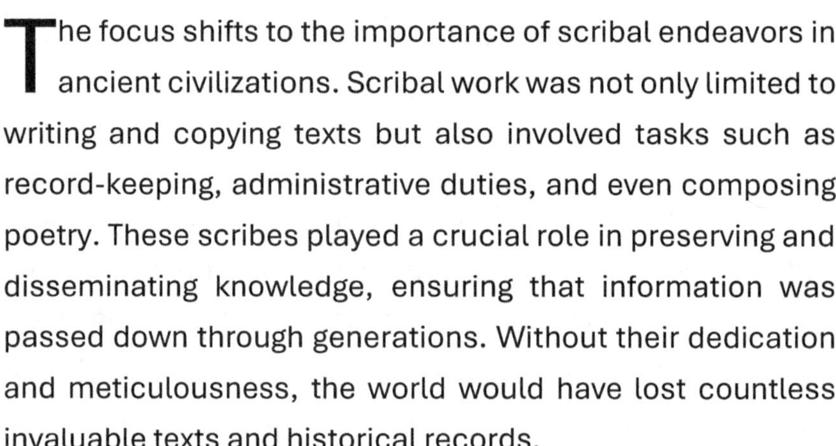

The focus shifts to the importance of scribal endeavors in ancient civilizations. Scribal work was not only limited to writing and copying texts but also involved tasks such as record-keeping, administrative duties, and even composing poetry. These scribes played a crucial role in preserving and disseminating knowledge, ensuring that information was passed down through generations. Without their dedication and meticulousness, the world would have lost countless invaluable texts and historical records.

## 6.1: Medieval Scribes

To have a complete appreciation for the construction of the Codex Gigas, we must comprehend the part that medieval scribes played and their importance in the creation of manuscripts. In an era before the invention of the printing press, individuals known as scribes served as the keepers of knowledge. They were accountable for the painstaking transcribing of writings, maintaining cultural traditions, and distributing information.

## The Importance of Scribes

The scribes of the Middle Ages were the unsung heroes of their day because of their critical role in maintaining and transferring knowledge. Their task took great physical exertion and demanded a high level of expertise, patience, and commitment. Scribes were responsible for copying and illuminating manuscripts creating books with aesthetic and practical elements.

**The Tradition of Manuscript Production:** Before the invention of the printing press in the 15th century, books were uncommon and expensive since they were generally crafted by hand. This practice continued until the printing press was invented. The principal hubs for creating manuscripts were monastic scriptoria, where scribes laboriously copied writings, much of the time in the monastic stillness.

**The Training of Scribes:** Training Scribes underwent severe training, starting their careers as apprentices until eventually becoming fully proficient in transcribing. They were taught to write in various scripts, how to prepare parchment or vellum, how to produce ink, and how to construct beautiful ornamentation. Completing this course could take several years.

## The Importance of Scribes to the Transmission of Culture and Information

The scribal activity was essential to medieval Europe's intellectual and cultural advancement, and its importance cannot be overstated. Because of their efforts, many important works, including religious and legal papers, scientific treatises, and ancient literature, could be preserved. In addition, scribes had a role in the progression of literacy and language standardization.

**Knowledge Preserved:** Ancient books were entrusted to the care of scribes, who were tasked with protecting them so that subsequent generations may read them and benefit from the knowledge of those who came before. Many important works of literature, philosophy, and science may not exist today if they hadn't been committed to preserving them for future generations.

**Illuminated Manuscripts:** Illuminators were painters who embellished manuscripts with detailed pictures and illuminations. Scribes frequently worked together with illuminators to create these works. The aesthetic appeal of the books was improved because of the inclusion of these visual features, facilitating better comprehension of the content.

# 6.2: The Scribe of the Codex Gigas

The scribe's identity responsible for the Codex Gigas, often known as the "scribe of the Devil's Bible," is still a perplexing riddle that has baffled historians, researchers, and fans for centuries. The problem surrounding the scribe's identity is a difficult task that requires a mix of historical study, the examination of handwriting, and an investigation into the broader context of the manuscript's use within medieval monasticism.

## The Challenge of Identification

It is not easy to determine which scribe was responsible for creating the Codex Gigas. Like many others of its period, the book does not have a colophon, a traditional inscription found after a manuscript. It typically identifies the scribe, the year the manuscript was completed, and the location where it was produced. Our knowledge of the text's history and the person responsible for its development is lacking as a result of this omission, which has created a gap in our comprehension.

Without a colophon or any other kind of explicit self-identification within the text, researchers are forced to determine the scribe's identity based only on circumstantial evidence, historical context, and an examination of the manuscript.

## Historical Clues and Hypotheses

During their research, academics have developed several ideas about the author of the Codex Gigas. These hypotheses use the historical setting in which the book was produced and investigate the cryptic clues hidden within the manuscript's pages.

**Monastic Origin:** Given that the Codex Gigas is thought to have been created inside a monastery, it is plausible to hypothesize that the scribe was probably a member of a monastic community. This is because the Codex Gigas' origin is considered monastic. In medieval Europe, monasteries served as centers of learning and scholarship; thus, monks were often among the best-educated members of the communities in which they lived.

The skills of transcribing, illumination, and book manufacturing were taught to monastic scribes throughout their training. Their commitment to the mission of conserving knowledge via the use of manuscripts was unrivaled. Because of this, it is possible that the person who wrote the Codex Gigas was a monk experienced in the rigorous requirements of monastic life and academic study.

**Multilingual Competence:** One of the most noteworthy features of the Codex Gigas is the scribe's outstanding command of Latin, which can be seen throughout the contents of the text. This is one of the most impressive parts of the Codex Gigas. Latin was the language of academic and religious discourse in Europe throughout the Middle Ages, and it was also the language most widely used to create manuscripts.

The scribe likely has a high degree of education and experience, given that they can easily handle Latin. In addition, the manuscript includes various materials, including historical, religious, and medicinal information. This scribe's ability to communicate in many languages may indicate a well-rounded education, which was not unusual for monastic academics in that era.

**Dedication to the Task:** The production of the Codex Gigas was a colossal project that called for unyielding devotion and a steadfast focus on the work at hand. The incredible degree of devotion and persistence shown by the scribe may be inferred from the enormous size and intricacy of the book and the exquisite pictures it contains.

The mythical story of a monk condemned to have his life taken away by being sealed in a wall while he was still alive and who did the work to save his own adds a layer of mystery to the scribe's reasons for writing the Codex Gigas. The scribe was unwaveringly determined to finish this exceptional text, and one can only speculate as to what was driving him: desperation, atonement, or a feeling of responsibility.

## The Influence of Human Nature on the Content of the Manuscript

It is essential to remember that the Codex Gigas, despite the air of mystique and folklore surrounding it, is at its core a result of the work and competence of human beings. The meticulous labor of the scribe or scribes responsible for the development of the manuscript may be hidden behind its magnificent pages.

**The Handwriting Analysis:** One method for determining who the scribe was entails thoroughly examining the scribe's handwriting. Paleography, often called handwriting analysis, is a specialist research branch investigating ancient manuscripts' script, letter shapes, and calligraphic properties.

The script used in the Codex Gigas may be compared to other known instances of medieval handwriting from the same time period and geographic location if scholars carefully examine the script used in the Codex Gigas. This comparison examination may show commonalities or distinguishing aspects that might lead to a better understanding of the writer's identity.

**The Visual Clues:** The Codex Gigas has graphic features that, in addition to the text, give more insights into the talents and style of the scribe. The accuracy of the writing, the arrangement of the pages, and the creative aspects such as pictures, illuminations, and ornamental embellishments are all included in these visual cues.

The amount of artistry shown by the scribe and their aesthetic sensibility may be inferred from the level of detail, creative complexity, and consistency displayed in the visual aspects of the book. The search for possible matches may be more manageable if these components are compared to those found in other texts from the same period.

## The Legacy of the Scribe

Through their work on this magnificent book, the scribe of the Codex Gigas has left behind a legacy that will never be forgotten, regardless of whether or not they are identified. Their body of work continues to enthrall academics, historians, and amateurs alike and to be a source of inspiration for all. It serves as a tribute to the lasting power of the written word and the commitment of those who struggled to preserve knowledge at a period when books were scarce and valuable. This is because it serves as a testament to the continuing power of the written word.

The search for the identity of the scribe is still underway. This search is driven by the desire to shed light on the human tale behind the Codex Gigas and to obtain a greater understanding of the motives that prompted the creation of this persistent mystery.

In Chapter 6, we dig into the world of medieval scribes

and their essential role in the creation, preservation, and diffusion of information. In addition, it investigates the enigma surrounding the scribe responsible for the Codex Gigas, offering insight into the difficulties and theories associated with their identification. This chapter contributes significantly to the overall comprehension of how the text came to be and the human influence behind its unique pages.

Chapter 7

# Sacred and Secular

Our exploration of the Codex Gigas has led us through its confusing contents, mysterious scribe, and the time-honored monastic practices from which it originated. This chapter is a riveting trip into the heart of this unique book. This voyage will expose its dual nature as both a revered repository of holy writings and a vessel holding unusual and often troubling material. This journey will reveal its dual nature as a vessel sheltering unconventional and sometimes uncomfortable content. As we make our way through the pages of this chapter, we will disentangle the complicated dance inside the Codex Gigas between the holy and the profane.

## 7.1: The Religious Significance: A Gateway to the Divine

The Codex Gigas is a religious manuscript, as shown by the fact that its folios are decorated with vast excerpts from

55

the Latin Bible and liturgical writings. On these pages, we uncover the crucial function that the book plays as a guiding light in religious practice and as a cornerstone in the life of a devoted person.

## Liturgical Use: A Precious Companion

The role of liturgical companion was the principal purpose for which the Codex Gigas was created. During the Divine Office, a hallowed cycle of devotion woven into the fabric of monastic living was the trustworthy vessel from which monks got their daily nourishment of prayers, hymns, and psalms. This text was more than ink on parchment; it was the essential pulse of monastic liturgy, establishing the tempo for spiritual life.

**The Liturgical Calendar (A Travel Guide Through Time):** A liturgical calendar interspersed throughout the book's pages governed the ebb and flow of the Christian year. Monks followed the liturgical calendar's feasts and seasons to record vital religious events such as Christ's birth, saints' death, and other important religious occasions. The Codex Gigas directed their ethereal journey through time, which served as a heavenly compass for them.

## A Connection to the Divine: Beyond Mere Words

The Codex Gigas is more than just a liturgical guidebook; it is an actual connection to the divine. Every page, when lighted with the required laborious skill, turned into a doorway to the holy. Every word, as well as every stroke of the pen, represented an act of dedication. This text served as more than simply an object for devotion; it was the medium via which monks communicated with the divine.

**The Visual Experience (Where Devotion and Art Meet):** The Codex Gigas used a visual symphony to enhance worship rather than relying entirely on words to accomplish this goal. Biblical characters and settings were brought to life via the use of illuminations. These vivid visual storylines, full of rich symbolism, were not only ornamental ornaments but also served as portals to a higher level of spiritual transcendence.

**An Item Deserving of Worship (The Sacred Presence Within):** Within the confines of the monastery, the Codex Gigas served as a book and a holy relic. Awe and reverence were instilled in all who saw it due to its enormous size, meticulous artistry, and rumors about its miraculous beginnings. Not only did monks read from it, but they also treasured it as a precious item since it was seen as a gateway to the divine.

# 7.2: The Darker Side: Unconventional and Controversial

A layer of the Codex Gigas shrouded in mystery questions the traditional religious standards and ventures into uncharted territory. This layer may be found buried under the surface of the book's apparent religiosity. This part is an in-depth exploration of the most mysterious and, at times, contentious aspects of the book.

## The Inclusion of Unusual Texts: A Shrouded Mystery

Texts deviating from the conventional canon of religious scripture are included in the Codex Gigas, one of the most fascinating aspects of this ancient book. These sections include rites and information that push the bounds of what may be called orthodox, going beyond what is found in the Bible and liturgy.

**The Spiritual Warfare Behind the Art of Exorcism:** Exorcism rites are given primary focus inside the Codex Gigas, despite this subject being often consigned to the periphery of religious discourse. Instructions and prayers for casting out demons and evil spirits are included in these ceremonies, which were documented with great attention to detail. The book focuses on the supernatural rather than being avoided like the plague in other versions.

**The Heptameron of Peter of Abano: Delving into the Occult:** The presence of the Heptameron, which is a grimoire or book of magic spells and rites and is said to have been written by Peter of Abano, is also perplexing. This section of the text delves into the occult by providing instructions on calling upon angels and devils, a subject area not often seen in religious documents.

# Debates and Controversies: A Matter of Interpretation

The fact that the Codex Gigas contains several unconventional passages has given rise to heated arguments and conflicts among academics and religious leaders. Some believe these aspects are evidence of a more varied approach to spirituality. Some people see them as inconsistencies within the framework of religion, which has sparked a heated debate among intellectuals.

**A Search for Knowledge: Finding Your Way Through Complexity:** It is necessary to analyze the intellectual landscape of the medieval era to understand these atypical characteristics. The intellectuals and philosophers of the period investigated a broad range of topics, often going beyond the confines of orthodox religious dogma. Even within the context of religious organizations, it was not unheard of for people to pursue studies in natural philosophy, astrology, and the occult.

**The Reason Behind the Manuscript: Going Beyond What Is Already Known**: The fact that the Codex Gigas contains information that is not typical raises the following question: What exactly was the intention behind it? Was it supposed to be an all-encompassing compilation of knowledge that brought together religious and secular enlightenment? Or did it have a more specific purpose, such as assisting in performing rituals involving magic or exorcism?

## The Complexity of Belief: A Multifaceted Tapestry

The Codex Gigas is an invitation to acknowledge and appreciate the complex nature of religion and spirituality in the world of the Middle Ages. It questions categorizations that are too simple, such as religious vs. secular. It reveals the fluidity of intellectual and spiritual borders in a society where knowledge was still developing.

**The Quest for Understanding: An Ongoing Odyssey:** As we go through the Codex Gigas, let us do it with our minds and hearts open to the material. Let us go through its unorthodox material together, remembering that searching for knowledge and spirituality is an intricate and diverse trip. The book encourages us to be open to various viewpoints and interpretations, demonstrating how the fabric of human thinking and belief constantly shifts and develops.

In Chapter 7, we set sail on an exciting journey into the heart of the Codex Gigas, where we find its dual identity as both a holy repository and a storehouse of unorthodox knowledge. This chapter takes us deep into the core of the Codex Gigas. Within its pages, it encourages us to investigate the subtle dance between the holy and the secular; it is a cryptic story that never ceases to enchant and mystify.

# Chapter 8

# Codex in Transit

During our journey through the Codex Gigas, we encountered its religious importance, looked into its unorthodox characteristics, and investigated the mystery surrounding its scribe. In this chapter, we set out on a trip through history that will follow the movements of the text as it was passed down through the years. This astonishing voyage illustrates the physical peregrinations of the Codex Gigas, the historical events it observed, and the precautions that were taken to guarantee that it would be preserved for future generations.

## 8.1: Historical Journey: From Monastery to Library

The fact that the Codex Gigas has survived the test of time is evidence of its continuing importance and the intrigue it has inspired. This part takes us on a journey through history, illuminating the course taken by the manuscript from the time it was created inside a monastery to the present day when it is housed in libraries and other institutions around Europe.

## Birthplace: The Monastery of Podlažice

Our adventure starts at the Monastery of Podlaice, located in Podlaice, in the center of medieval Bohemia. According to legend, the Codex Gigas was first written down here. We go further into the historical fabric of this monastery, tracing its part in the production of the text as well as the importance of the monastic community that formerly resided there.

**The Monastery's Historical Background: A Center of Learning:** As was the case with many other monastic institutions of its day, the Monastery of Podlaice served as a center of study and knowledge. It was a location where monks devoted their lives to the quest for knowledge, and it was also a site where manuscripts such as the Codex Gigas were painstakingly made.

**The Life Within Monastic Routines:** We fully immerse ourselves in the routine activities of the monks living inside the monastery so that we may appreciate the setting in which the Codex Gigas was created. We investigate their daily rituals, the stringent religious practices they followed, and their spartan lives—a life characterized by commitment and self-control.

## A Journey Beyond the Monastery: Changing Hands

As the Codex Gigas journeyed through history, it went through several different owners' hands, moving through a complex web of historical moments and geographic locales. This section outlines its voyage and draws attention to the critical occurrences that were significant landmarks along the way.

**Dispersal of Monastic Treasures: Turbulent Times:** The stormy events of history had a significant impact on the route that the text took. Throughout history, monasteries have often been at risk of destruction by war and other forms of social upheaval. Many monastery valuables, like the Codex Gigas, were scattered and moved to several locations for storage.

**The Habsburg Connection: Royal Ownership:** Our travels lead us to the very center of the Habsburg Empire, where the mighty Habsburg kings were in control of the Codex Gigas and where they first acquired it. In this section, we investigate the function that the manuscript plays as an essential asset within the royal collection and its relevance within the framework of imperial authority.

**Relocation to Sweden: A Twist of Fate:** The voyage of the Codex Gigas involves an exciting turn of events: the transfer of the text from the Habsburgs to the Swedes amid the turmoil of the Thirty Years' War. We investigate the events that led up to this transfer as well as the significance of the text to the cultural and historical legacy of Sweden.

## 8.2: Preservation and Protection: Safeguarding a Treasure

It is a monument to the efforts undertaken to conserve and defend this priceless resource. The remarkable survival of the Codex Gigas through centuries of wars, upheavals, and shifting governments has been preserved and protected. In this part, we will learn about the field of manuscript conservation and the procedures carried out to protect the Codex Gigas.

### Guardians of Knowledge: Libraries and Institutions

Throughout its travels, the Codex Gigas sought solace at several libraries and other establishments. In this section, we explore the relevance of these information reservoirs and the role they played in protecting the document.

**The Royal Library of Sweden: A New Home:** Because of its time spent in Sweden, the Codex Gigas is now housed at the Royal Library of Sweden, which is considered an essential component of the national collection. In this article, we investigate the significance that the manuscript plays in Sweden's cultural history and its influence on academic endeavors.

**Challenges of Preservation: The Manuscript's Condition:** The state of the manuscript is as follows: Keeping a text of the grandeur of the Codex Gigas safe for future generations was no easy task. The vellum degrades with time, and the ink and the pages become less legible. We look at the difficulties that conservators encounter while trying to preserve the originality of a text.

## Modern Conservation Efforts: The Role of Technology

Even in this day and age of rapidly advancing technology, the Codex Gigas maintains its status as a topic of interest and research. We explore the contemporary conservation efforts that have been made, such as imaging and scientific analysis, and the contributions that these efforts have made to our knowledge of the document's origins, materials, and validity.

**Imaging Techniques: Peering into the Past:** Researchers have been able to look behind the surface of the Codex Gigas, uncovering previously unknown features and gaining new perspectives on how it was created due to their efforts. To unravel the riddles in the document, we investigate the use of multispectral imaging in addition to other methodologies.

**Scientific Analysis: Unraveling the Manuscript's Secrets:** The manuscript's content and its historical setting have been better-understood thanks to the findings of many scientific analyses, such as those on the ink and the parchment. This section looks into the scientific achievements that have contributed to our enhanced comprehension of the Codex Gigas.

# 8.3: A Living Relic: The Codex's Enduring Allure

Because of its long and winding path through history, the Codex Gigas is now considered a living relic in the modern day. This section considers the continuing appeal of the manuscript, its role in popular culture and literature, and its capacity to grab the imagination of individuals of all eras and from all walks of life.

## An Icon in Popular Culture: Literary and Media Presence

The importance of the Codex Gigas as just a text has been eclipsed by its status as a symbol in contemporary popular culture. We investigate its appearance in books, movies, and other forms of media, where it has and continues to spark imagination and curiosity among audiences.

**Literary Works: A Muse for Authors:** The mysterious nature of the Codex Gigas has been a source of creativity for writers who have included it in their works. We dig into works of literature that highlight the manuscript and its function as a source of inspiration for creative minds.

## Cultural and Religious Impact: Beyond Its Pages

The parchment and ink that make up the pages of the Codex Gigas are just a tiny part of the legacy left by this book. We investigate its enduring relevance in global cultural and religious history, its contributions to our knowledge of the medieval world, and its influence on religious studies and historical study.

**A Window into the Past: Insights from the Codex:** The manuscript provides a unique insight into the world of the Middle Ages, illuminating for us the beliefs, knowledge, and creative sensitivities of the people who lived during that period. We take time to reflect on the knowledge we obtained from the Codex Gigas and its function as an essential historical item.

**The Codex in Academic Discourse: A Subject of Study:** The contents and historical background of the Codex Gigas are still being investigated as part of the researchers' ongoing research into the Codex Gigas. We investigate the academic debate surrounding the manuscript and how it continues to be necessary for studying the Middle Ages.

As we end our exploration of Chapter 8, we pause to contemplate the incredible trip that the Codex Gigas has taken. This manuscript has been a part of history for hundreds of years, from when it was written down at the

Podlaice Monastery to its current location in contemporary libraries. We are left with an incredible feeling of wonder and interest in this unique document due to its continuing attractiveness as both a holy relic and a source of mystery. This allure has not faded through time.

In Chapter 8, we started on an enthralling voyage through time, tracking the route of the Codex Gigas from its beginnings in a monastery to its present-day position as an everlasting relic. This was a fascinating adventure through time. This text continues to capture hearts and minds, which is a monument to the continuing power of knowledge and the endurance of cultural treasures over the years. The manuscript has a rich history, and it also has a mysterious presence.

◆◆◆◆◆◆◆◆◆

# Chapter 9

# Modern Investigations

As we go farther into the core of the Codex Gigas, our trip will take a turn toward the modern-day beginning in Chapter 9. In this chapter, we go into the contemporary period, where a confluence of technology breakthroughs and intellectual inquiries have played a crucial part in uncovering the mysteries contained inside the document. From recent research initiatives to cutting-edge scientific studies, we set out on an exciting adventure of discovery to excavate a better knowledge of the mysterious Codex Gigas. This trip will take us from recent research endeavors to cutting-edge scientific analysis.

## 9.1: Contemporary Studies: A New Lens

The Codex Gigas is now being analyzed from a fresh perspective due to the advent of the digital era. This section analyzes how the manuscript has been a focus point for modern studies, offering light on new research, analyses, and results that have contributed to our expanding grasp of this fantastic work. Specifically, this part examines how the manuscript has become a focal point for contemporary studies.

## The Codex Gigas in the Digital Era

The introduction of the digital age has brought about a profound change in how we interact with ancient manuscripts such as the Codex Gigas. We will go into how current technology, such as digital photography and the construction of enormous archive databases, has altered the accessibility of this book, as well as the extent of the study that can be done on it.

**Digitization Initiatives: Unlocking the Manuscript's Secrets:** Several digitalization efforts have been started to make the Codex Gigas more accessible to academics all around the globe. We will investigate how digital photographs with a high resolution have made it possible for academics to examine the text at a level of unparalleled detail, removing the geographical obstacles that formerly kept scholars at a distance from this priceless historical artifact.

## Insights from Multidisciplinary Approaches

It is necessary to use a multidisciplinary approach to decipher the secrets inside the Codex Gigas. This approach should integrate historical, linguistic, and scientific approaches. In this study, we will analyze how multidisciplinary techniques have been used to provide fresh light on the manuscript's origins, materials, and the historical environment in which it was created.

**Linguistic Analysis: Deciphering the Manuscript's Language:** Linguists have studied the language used inside the Codex Gigas and have uncovered some beneficial information about the scribe who wrote it and the linguistic influences that were prevalent during that period. In this section, we will investigate the critical role of linguistic analysis in interpreting the often obscure material contained within the book.

**Scientific Analysis: Materials and Preservation:** The scientific study results, which included in-depth investigations into the make-up of the ink and the characteristics of the parchment, have revealed essential insights into the construction and preservation of the Codex Gigas. We will dig into how these scientific investigations have extended our understanding of the physical characteristics of the document as well as the complex procedures that led to its production.

## 9.2: The Codex Gigas in the 21st Century: New Perspectives

The voyage of the Codex Gigas does not come to an end in the past; instead, it continues into the current day, where it continues to be significant in both the academic and cultural worlds. This part investigates the manuscript's function in modern scholarship and its position in a world that is changing quickly.

## The Manuscript as Cultural Heritage

The Codex Gigas is a significant historical and cultural treasure, giving it a place in history that is unmatched. Even though the world is in perpetual flux, we will investigate how it helps maintain our cultural legacy and cultivates a feeling of continuity with the past.

**Exhibitions and Public Engagement:** The manuscript's fascination stretches far beyond academia, catching the imagination of the general people. In this session, we will investigate how public engagement programs and exhibits have made the Codex Gigas accessible to a larger audience, therefore stimulating curiosity and interest in the history and culture of the Middle Ages.

## Ongoing Research and Lingering Questions

Even after centuries of research, the Codex Gigas still has many interesting questions and puzzles that have not been solved. We will dive into the current research efforts and academic arguments surrounding the text. These discussions include queries regarding the authorship of the book, as well as its purpose and broader importance.

**Authorship: The Elusive Scribe**

A mystery surrounds the identity of the scribe responsible for writing the Codex Gigas. In this section, we will investigate the many speculations and theories advanced by academics to shed light on the enduring enigma surrounding the scribe's identity.

**Purpose and Significance: A Multifaceted Manuscript**

The complex structure of the document raises issues regarding the goals that it was designed to accomplish. We will investigate the many interpretations of the meaning of the Codex Gigas. These interpretations range from the Codex Gigas being a complete storehouse of information to it playing specialized functions in certain rites.

# 9.3: The Codex Gigas in a Global Context

The value of the Codex Gigas extends well beyond its roots in the Czech Republic, making it a worldwide treasure with far-reaching effects. In this part, we are going to investigate its location in a global context by looking at the impact that it has had on historical studies, religious studies, and the cultural comprehension of people all around the globe.

**Medieval Europe and Beyond**

The Codex Gigas provides a one-of-a-kind look into medieval Europe and the larger cultural and theological environment that existed during that period. We will discuss how it deepens our comprehension of medieval ways of living, spirituality, and intellectual pursuits and how it resonates with audiences in locations far different from where it was first developed.

## Religious Studies: A Multifaceted Manuscript

The fact that the document contains material outside of the norm, religiously speaking, challenges those bounds. We will dive into its significance in the study of religious history, its influence on theological discourse, and its function in sculpting our comprehension of different belief systems.

## Cultural Exchange: A Manuscript Across Borders

The journey that the Codex Gigas has taken through history has taken it to many different places and cultures. We will investigate how the manuscript's journeys have promoted cultural interaction and fostered a more profound awareness of the history that all people share.

## A Continuing Odyssey

As we conclude our trip through Chapter 9, we take some time to think about the Codex Gigas' continued significance in today's world. This document continues to be a symbol of human curiosity, study, and the never-ending effort to discover the hidden truths of the past, whether it be in the context of modern studies or cultural engagement.

In Chapter 9, we are allowed to go on a journey into the current research surrounding the Codex Gigas. Along the way, we will discover how cutting-edge technology and diverse methods have taken us closer to deciphering its secrets. This text continues to capture hearts and minds, which is a monument to the continuing power of knowledge and the endurance of cultural treasures over the years. The manuscript has a rich history, and it also has a mysterious presence.

Chapter 10

# Legacy of the Enigma

As we prepare to go on the last part of our adventure through the mysterious worlds of the Codex Gigas, we discover that we have entered the domain of its legacy. This legacy spans generations and is independent of both time and culture. The fascination of this remarkable text is shown to have withstood the test of time in Chapter 10. Despite the passage of time, the Codex Gigas continues to be an object of interest and mystery, and it continues to capture the hearts and minds of people all over the globe. We investigate its place in popular culture and literature, its tremendous influence on the study of religion and historical inquiry, and its lasting mark on successive generations.

## 10.1: The Enduring Allure

The mysticism surrounding the Codex Gigas is a mystery in and of itself. In this part, we will investigate the enduring appeal of the text, which has withstood the ravages of both the passage of time and the advancement of technology. Even in this fast-paced and technological era of the 21st century, we want to comprehend why this mysterious piece of art continues to be such a fascinating topic of study.

## An Icon in Popular Culture: A Literary and Media Presence

The life of the Codex Gigas has progressed much beyond that of a simple manuscript, entering the worlds of literature, cinema, television, and other forms of popular culture along the way. In this article, we investigate its existence in these many kinds of creative expression, where it has provided a source of inspiration for storytellers throughout generations. These forms of creative expression have been passed down from generation to generation.

**Literary Works: An Enigmatic Muse:** The Codex Gigas has motivated writers from various periods who have incorporated the book's enigmas into their stories. This section uncovers literary works that include the manuscript, illuminating its function as a muse for creative minds who have enhanced the world of narrative by using its persistent mystery. The works are uncovered to provide light on its role as a muse for creative minds.

**Film and Television: The Codex on Screen:** The Codex Gigas has been included in several films and television shows, often playing parts evocating the mysterious reputation it has earned. We investigate its appearances in various forms of visual storytelling and investigate how its existence has contributed to the attractiveness of various visual storytelling media.

### Cultural Icon: A Symbol of Intrigue

The Codex Gigas has developed into a cultural symbol in addition to playing a significant part in popular culture. We investigate the symbolism it carries and its role in creating the cultural imagination, not just in its native area but also in other parts of the world.

**Cultural Significance: A Revered Artifact:** As a respected relic, the Codex Gigas holds a distinctive position in Czech culture since it is considered a respected relic that reflects the nation's rich historical and intellectual history. We dive into its importance within Czech society, which promotes a feeling of national pride and cultural connection, and we do so to understand it better.

## 10.2: Cultural and Religious Impact

The impact of the Codex Gigas is felt well beyond the bounds of its pages, leaving an enduring imprint on both the cultural and religious landscapes. In this part, we investigate its enduring relevance in the history of culture and religion, illuminating its contributions to our understanding of the medieval world.

## The Codex Gigas as a Historical Artifact

The text serves as a gateway to the past and provides a one-of-a-kind look into the way of life, philosophy, and spirituality throughout the Middle Ages. We consider its significance as an irreplaceable historical relic and how it has added to our understanding of ancient times as we do so.

**Insights into Medieval Life: A Time Capsule:** The Codex Gigas acts as a time capsule, preserving the beliefs and knowledge of medieval society and its aesthetic sensibility. We delve into the many facets of medieval life, such as religion, science, and culture, to get the priceless insights this text offers.

## Impact on Religious Studies

The presence of unorthodox material in the Codex Gigas challenges traditional religious practice's established norms and bounds. We investigate its influence on the academic discipline of religious studies, its place in theological conversation, and the disputes it has sparked among academics and theologians.

**Theological Debates: Challenging Norms:** The document contains material in certain areas that question the legitimacy of established religious canons. In this article, we investigate the arguments and controversies surrounding these components of the Codex Gigas and the consequences these characteristics have for the study of religion.

# 10.3: A Living Relic

The Codex Gigas is not even close to being a relic from the past; it continues to be a source of amazement, interest, and the quest for knowledge today. In this part of the article, we investigate its ever-present nature in the 21st century and its capacity to stimulate curiosity and discovery.

## Continued Scholarship

The Codex Gigas is still being investigated by academics from all over the globe, who are looking into its contents, historical context, and mysteries. We dive into the current scholarly debate surrounding the document and emphasize the manuscript's significance in the context of modern study.

**Contemporary Studies: Advancements and Inquiries:** This article investigates how technological advances and multidisciplinary research have contributed to a deeper comprehension of the Codex Gigas. This mystery dates back hundreds of years and has been the subject of recent investigations, which have provided new insights and viewpoints on the topic. As a result, it continues to serve as a fruitful ground for intellectual study.

## A Legacy for Future Generations

The Codex Gigas is not a relic that will eventually become obsolete; it is a living heritage handed down through the years. As we consider its lasting significance in education and the protection of cultural heritage for future generations, we ensure that the secrets contained within the text will continue to captivate and intrigue people.

## An Eternal Enigma

As we conclude our journey through Chapter 10, we are in awe of the lasting legacy of the Codex Gigas. This document, with its long history, complex nature, and enduring attractiveness, is a tribute to humanity's unquenchable hunger for knowledge and our ageless fascination with the secrets of the past. Its history dates back centuries, and its nature is complex and multidimensional.

This magnificent manuscript continues to fascinate hearts and minds in the 21st century, as shown in Chapter 10, which submerges us in the enduring attraction of the Codex Gigas. It serves as a helpful reminder that certain mysteries will always be with us, posing a never-ending challenge to seek knowledge and investigate the breadth and depth of human curiosity.

# Conclusion

## The Codex Gigas - A Tale of Enigma, Intrigue, and Enduring Mystery

In the annals of history, many manuscripts have attained legendary status. Among them, the Codex Gigas reigns as a monument to the lasting strength of the written word and the insatiable human quest for knowledge. The Codex Gigas is a tribute to the staying power of the written word and the insatiable human thirst for knowledge. Our trip through this magnificent document has been nothing short of an odyssey—examining mystery, intrigue, and the age-old secrets of the past. This adventure began with the production of the text and ended with its legacy in the contemporary day. In this extensive conclusion, we consider the relevance of the Codex Gigas, its nature as a complex entity, and its deep mark on the world.

### Unveiling the Codex Gigas: A Journey of Discovery

The start of our journey was marked by the discovery of the Codex Gigas, which was hidden away in the Sedlec

Monastery in Bohemia. We investigated the awe-inspiring physical characteristics of this monumental text, marveling at its sheer size, meticulous binding, and vellum pages that have resisted the ravages of time. It was clear that the Codex Gigas was more than just a book; it was a monument to human achievement and a testimony to the painstaking artistry of medieval scribes.

## Chapter 1: The Legend Begins

Our travels took us further into the tales and traditions associated with the text, which is how the Codex Gigas became known as the "Bible of the Devil." A spell of intrigue has been put upon us by tales of magical beginnings, a scribe's deal with the devil, and the sheer impossibility of its production in a single night. All these things add up to make the book's creation impossible. We were astounded by how history and tradition had been woven together to create a written document into a mysterious myth.

## Chapter 2: A Monumental Manuscript

The second part took us into the material world of the Codex Gigas, where we investigated its dimensions, mass, and the laborious artistry that went into its production. The difficulties that medieval scribes had while preparing parchment, creating ink, and transcribing complex manuscripts provided light on the level of commitment necessary to execute such a monumental work.

## Chapter 3: The Art of the Devil

The third part delves into the notorious devil's picture inside the Codex Gigas, elucidating the symbolism and iconography linked with the devil in art created throughout the Middle Ages. As a result of our exploration of the historical and cultural milieu in which the devil was portrayed throughout the Middle Ages, we now have a better understanding of how people during that period saw, feared, and represented him.

## Chapter 4: Echoes from the Monastery

Our search brought us to the Monastery of Podlaice, which is said to be the location where the Codex Gigas was first written down. We investigated the history of the monastery, its location, and its role in the globe throughout the Middle Ages. In addition, we immersed ourselves in the everyday lives of monks during the construction of the Codex. This allowed us to understand better the atmosphere in which this unique document was allegedly written.

## Chapter 5: Beyond the Bible

In Chapter 5, the contents of the Codex Gigas were revealed, and a comprehensive analysis of the numerous passages inside its pages was provided. We went through historical and medical writings that were not as well recognized as well as religious texts like the Bible. The book's mystery was enhanced by the fact that it included a wide variety of material, which led to questioning its intended use outside the confines of religious writings.

## Chapter 6: Scribal Endeavors

In Chapter 6, we continued our exploration of the importance of medieval scribes and the roles they played. We gained an understanding of the education and experience necessary for these scribes, as well as an appreciation for the crucial role they played in preserving information throughout the medieval period. The fact that the identity of the scribe responsible for the Codex Gigas has been shrouded in mystery has further helped to humanize this gigantic work.

## Chapter 7: Sacred and Secular

The role of the Codex Gigas in religious rites church activities, and its significance in medieval Christianity were discussed in Chapter 7. This chapter also examined how the Codex Gigas straddled the worlds of religion. While we were reading the book, we came across several unorthodox and contentious parts. These features challenged the accepted religious standards of the day and sparked heated controversy.

## Chapter 8: Codex in Transit

In Chapter 8, we embarked on a voyage through history, following the path of the text as it traveled throughout Europe over many centuries. We were able to trace the history of the Codex Gigas and learn how it passed through several monasteries and libraries while bearing witness to various historical occurrences. In addition, we were given information on the efforts taken to preserve and guard this priceless document.

## Chapter 9: Modern Investigations

After completing Chapter 9, we entered the contemporary period, an era in which the Codex Gigas has been reexamined in light of new technical developments and multidisciplinary perspectives. We investigated modern investigations, scientific assessments, and the continuous existence of the document in cultural and religious debate. It became abundantly clear that the voyage of the Codex Gigas was not even close to being finished; it continued to encourage study and discovery.

## Chapter 10: Legacy of the Enigma

Chapter 10 was the pinnacle of our journey, during which we reflected on the enduring legacy that the Codex Gigas has left behind. We investigated its enduring appeal, its place in contemporary society, and the influence it has had on the fields of religious studies and historical study. This mysterious document came to be seen as a symbol of humanity's never-ending effort to satisfy its insatiable curiosity, advance academia, and decipher the mysteries of the past.

# The Codex Gigas: A Multifaceted Masterpiece

The Codex Gigas is a multidimensional work that transcends its status as a holy document to become a tribute to human success, creativity, and the unquenchable desire for knowledge. It is a masterpiece that is a testament to human achievement, creativity, and the unquenchable pursuit of knowledge. It is a storehouse of history, culture, and spirituality, providing a glimpse into the Middle Ages world.